NOW YOU CAN READ....

The Ugly Duckling

STORY ADAPTED BY LUCY KINCAID

ILLUSTRATED BY GILLIAN EMBLETON

BRIMAX BOOKS • CAMBRIDGE • ENGLAND

Mother Duck had five broken egg shells, and five new ducklings. She had one egg which did not have a crack in it.

"I wonder when that egg will hatch," said Mother Duck.

Everyone who lived in the farmyard
came to look at the egg.
"That is too big to be a duck's
egg," said a chicken.
"That will hatch into a turkey,
you mark my words," said a goose.
"How will I know if it is a
turkey?" asked Mother Duck.
"It will not swim," said the
goose.

At last the egg hatched. The bird which stepped from the broken shell did not look like his brothers and sisters at all. But he was not a turkey for he went straight to the pond and began to swim.

"What an ugly little duckling you are," laughed the chickens.

"What an ugly little duckling you are," laughed the geese.
"What an ugly little duckling you are," laughed the other ducks.

The little duckling was so unhappy.
He had no friends. EVERYONE laughed
at him, even his mother.
He decided to run away. "Nobody
will miss me," he said. And
nobody did.

He made his home on the marshes.
One day he saw some wild ducks
swimming in a pool. "Will you be
my friends?" he asked.
"What an ugly little duckling you
are," laughed the wild ducks. "We
do not want you in our pool."
They chased him away.

One day the little duckling saw
some swans flying across the sky.
"I wish I were a swan," he said.
"Swans are beautiful. Nobody laughs
at them." He felt sadder than
ever as he watched them fly away.

Winter came. The days were cold.
The nights were even colder. Food
was very hard to find.
Now the little duckling was not
only lonely, he was cold and
hungry too.

One cold night the lake froze.
When morning came the duckling's
feet were stuck firmly in the ice.
He could not move.
"Now I will die," he said.
A farmer was taking his dog for a
walk. He saw the duckling stuck
in the ice.
"We must get you out of there,"
he said.
The farmer broke the ice with a
stick. The little duckling was
free again.

"Go and find your friends," said the farmer.

"I wish I had a friend to find," said the little duckling sadly.

The winter was very long but it did not last for ever. Spring came. The days grew warmer. There was plenty to eat. The wild ducks and the wild geese came back to the lake. They had all been away for the winter.

They dabbled and they splashed
about in the water and all
tried to talk at once.
They had so many things to tell
one another. But nobody spoke to
the little duckling.
"I wish they would talk to me,"
he said.

The little duckling
watched the wild
ducks stretch their
wings. He
stretched his own wings.
He flapped them.
And then he flew,
for the very first
time. Up, up and
up, he went, up
into the clear blue
sky.

He should have been happy, but he did not feel happy. He looked down at the ground far below him. He could see the swans swimming in a pond in a beautiful garden. He would ask them to help him.

He flew down to the pond and settled on the water. He called to the swans. "Please come and kill me. I am so ugly, and I am so lonely I do not want to live."

"Ugly? You?" said the swans looking surprised. "Have you looked at yourself in the pond?"

The little duckling looked down into the water. Looking back at him was a swan.

"Is . . . is that me?" he asked.
"Of course it is," said the swans.
"But I am beautiful," he said.
"Of course you are," said the swans.
"You are a swan. All swans are beautiful."

Three children came running to the pond.

"Look!" they cried. "A new swan. Please stay in our pond. We will come and see you every day."

The little duckling had changed into a beautiful swan during the long cold winter. He would never be lonely again.

All these appear in the pages of the story. Can you find them?

Mother Duck

chicken

goose

duckling